Practical Guide

1.Introduction to Swift

Swift is a powerful and versatile programming language developed by Apple Inc. It was first introduced in 2014 as a replacement for Objective-C and quickly became the go-to language for iOS and macOS development. In this article, we will provide an introduction to Swift, exploring its features, syntax, and benefits.

One of the key features of Swift is its readability. The syntax of Swift is designed to be clear and concise, making it easier to write and understand code. This makes it an excellent choice for both experienced developers and beginners. Additionally, Swift is known for its safety features, such as type inference and optionals, which help prevent common programming errors.

Another advantage of Swift is its performance. Swift is a fast and efficient language, thanks to its modern design and optimized compiler. This makes it ideal for building high-performance applications that run smoothly on a variety of devices. In fact, many developers have reported significant performance improvements when switching from Objective-C to Swift.

Furthermore, Swift is a versatile language that can be used for a wide range of applications. In addition to iOS and macOS development, Swift can also be used for server-side programming, thanks to the open-source SwiftNIO framework. This allows developers to write end-to-end Swift applications that can run on both client and server.

One of the standout features of Swift is its interoperability with Objective-C. This means that developers can seamlessly integrate Swift code into existing Objective-C projects, making it easier to transition to the new language. Additionally, Swift is fully compatible with Apple's Cocoa and Cocoa

Touch frameworks, allowing developers to leverage existing APIs and tools.

In terms of syntax, Swift is a modern and expressive language that borrows elements from various programming languages, such as Python, Ruby, and C#. This makes it easy to learn for developers who are familiar with these languages. Swift also introduces new concepts, such as optionals, closures, and generics, which provide additional flexibility and power.

One of the key benefits of Swift is its focus on safety and stability. The language includes features like optional chaining, nil coalescing, and guard statements, which help prevent common programming errors and improve code reliability. Additionally, Swift has strong type safety, which helps catch errors at compile time rather than runtime.

Swift also includes various modern

programming paradigms, such as functional programming and protocol-oriented programming. These paradigms allow developers to write cleaner, more modular code that is easier to test and maintain. Swift's support for generics also enables developers to write reusable code that can work with different types.

Overall, Swift is a versatile and powerful programming language that offers a wide range of benefits for developers. Whether you are a beginner looking to learn your first programming language or an experienced developer looking to build high-performance applications, Swift is a great choice. With its modern syntax, safety features, and performance optimizations, Swift is sure to remain a popular language for years to come.

2.Installing and Configuring the Swift Development Environment

Swift is a powerful and intuitive programming language developed by Apple for macOS, iOS, watchOS, and tvOS applications. With its modern syntax and concise yet expressive features, Swift has quickly become a favorite among developers for building cutting-edge applications.

In this article, we will explore the steps required to install and configure the Swift development environment on your machine. Whether you are a beginner looking to delve into the world of iOS development or a seasoned developer wanting to explore a new language, this guide will help you set up your environment quickly and efficiently.

Step 1: Download Xcode

Before we can start writing Swift code, we need to download Xcode, Apple's Integrated Development Environment (IDE) for macOS. Xcode is essential for writing, testing, and debugging Swift applications, as well as for deploying your apps to Apple's App Store.

To download Xcode, visit the Mac App Store and search for "Xcode." Once you have found the Xcode app, click on the download button and follow the on-screen instructions to install it on your machine. Xcode is a large file, so the download may take some time depending on your internet connection speed.

Step 2: Install Xcode Command Line Tools

After installing Xcode, we need to install the Xcode Command Line Tools. These tools provide additional functionality for developers, including compilers and other essential development tools.

To install the Xcode Command Line Tools, open the terminal on your Mac and type the following command:

```

xcode-select --install

```

Follow the on-screen instructions to complete the installation process. Once the command line tools are installed, you will have access to additional command-line utilities that will aid in your Swift development.

Step 3: Install Homebrew

Homebrew is a package manager for macOS that simplifies the process of installing software and libraries on your machine. To install Homebrew, open the terminal and paste the following command:

```
/bin/bash -c "$(curl -fsSL https://raw.githubusercontent.com/Homebrew/install/HEAD/install.sh)"
```

Follow the on-screen instructions to complete the installation process. Homebrew will be installed on your machine and ready to use for installing Swift-related tools and libraries.

Step 4: Install Swift

Now that we have Xcode, the Xcode Command Line Tools, and Homebrew installed, we can proceed to install the Swift programming language on our machine. With Homebrew, installing Swift is simple. In the terminal, type the following command:

```

brew install swift

```

The Homebrew package manager will download and install Swift on your machine. This may take some time depending on your internet connection speed, so be patient while the installation completes.

Step 5: Verify Swift Installation

To verify that Swift has been installed correctly on your machine, open the terminal and type:

```
```

```
swift --version
```

If Swift has been installed successfully, you will see the version number displayed in the terminal. This confirms that Swift is now installed and ready to use for development.

Step 6: Configure an IDE for Swift Development

While Xcode is the preferred IDE for Swift development, there are other options available for those who prefer a different development environment. Some popular alternatives include:

- Visual Studio Code: A lightweight and versatile IDE that supports syntax highlighting and code completion for Swift.

- AppCode: A dedicated IDE for macOS and

iOS development, with advanced features for Swift projects.

- Atom: A customizable text editor that supports Swift development with the installation of plugins.

- Sublime Text: A lightweight and flexible text editor that can be customized to support Swift development.

Choose the IDE that best suits your development style and preferences, and configure it for Swift development by installing any necessary plugins or extensions.

Step 7: Start Coding in Swift

With the Swift development environment set up on your machine, you are now ready to start coding in Swift. Create a new Swift project in your chosen IDE, and begin exploring the language's syntax and features.

Swift's modern syntax and powerful features make it a joy to work with, whether you are a seasoned developer or a beginner looking to learn a new language. Take advantage of Swift's ease of use and expressive capabilities to create innovative and engaging applications for Apple's platforms.

Installing and configuring the Swift development environment is a straightforward process that can be completed in just a few simple steps. By following the instructions outlined in this guide, you can set up your machine for Swift development and start coding in this powerful language in no time.

3.The Basics of Swift Language

Introduction

Swift is a powerful and intuitive programming language developed by Apple for building iOS, macOS, watchOS, and tvOS apps. It is designed to be easy to use, fast, and secure. In this article, we will explore the basics of the Swift language and get familiar with its key features.

Variables and Constants

In Swift, you can declare variables using the var keyword and constants using the let keyword. Variables can be changed after they are initialized, while constants cannot be changed once they are assigned a value. Here is an example of how you can declare a variable and a constant in Swift:

```swift
```

```
var myVariable = 10

let myConstant = "Hello, World!"
```

Data Types

Swift provides various data types such as Int (for integer values), Double (for floating-point values), String (for text), Bool (for boolean values), and more. You can also create your own custom data types using structures and classes. Here is an example of how you can declare variables of different data types in Swift:

```swift
var myInt: Int = 10

var myDouble: Double = 3.14

var myString: String = "Swift is awesome!"

var myBool: Bool = true
```

Control Flow

Swift provides several control flow statements such as if-else, switch-case, for-in, while, and repeat-while. You can use these statements to make decisions and repeat tasks based on certain conditions. Here is an example of how you can use the if-else statement in Swift:

```swift
var number = 10

if number % 2 == 0 {
    print("Even number")
} else {
    print("Odd number")
}
```

Functions

Functions in Swift are blocks of code that perform a specific task. You can define your own functions with or without parameters and return values. Here is an example of how you can create a simple function in Swift:

```swift
func greet(name: String) {
    print("Hello, \(name)!")
}

greet(name: "John")
```

Arrays and Dictionaries

Arrays and dictionaries are important data structures in Swift that allow you to store multiple values of the same type or key-value pairs, respectively. You can easily manipulate and access elements in arrays and dictionaries. Here is an example of how you can create an array and a dictionary in Swift:

```swift
var numbers = [1, 2, 3, 4, 5]

var names = ["John": 25, "Emily": 30, "Michael": 28]
```

Classes and Structures

Classes and structures are used to define custom data types in Swift. Classes are reference types, while structures are value types. You can create properties, methods, and initializers in classes and structures to encapsulate data and behaviors. Here is an example of how you can define a class and a structure in Swift:

```swift
```

```swift
class Person {

    var name: String

    var age: Int


    init(name: String, age: Int) {

        self.name = name

        self.age = age

    }

}


struct Point {

    var x: Int

    var y: Int

}
```

Optionals

Optionals are a special feature in Swift that allow you to handle the absence of a value. An optional variable can either have a value or be nil, which signifies that it does not have a value. You can use optional binding, optional chaining, and forced unwrapping to work with optionals. Here is an example of how you can use optionals in Swift:

```swift
var optionalName: String? = "John"

if let name = optionalName {

    print("Hello, \(name)!")

} else {

    print("Hello, stranger!")

}
```

In this article, we have covered the basics of the Swift language, including variables, constants, data types, control flow, functions, arrays, dictionaries, classes, structures, and optionals. Swift is a modern and versatile language that is widely used for iOS app development. By mastering these fundamentals, you will be well on your way to becoming a proficient Swift programmer.

4.Basic data types in Swift include variables and constants

Swift is a powerful and versatile programming language developed by Apple for iOS, macOS, watchOS, and tvOS. One of its core features is its rich support for different data types, which are essential for storing and manipulating information in a program. In this article, we will explore the fundamental data types in Swift, including variables, constants, and more.

Variables and Constants:

In Swift, variables are used to store mutable data, which can be changed throughout the execution of a program. Constants, on the other hand, are used to store immutable data, which cannot be changed after their initial assignment. Both variables and constants are declared using the var and let keywords, respectively.

Here is an example of declaring a variable and a constant in Swift:

```swift
var myVariable = 10

let myConstant = "Hello, World!"
```

In the above example, myVariable is a variable that stores an integer value of 10, while myConstant is a constant that stores a string value of "Hello, World!". Once a value is assigned to a constant, it cannot be changed.

Data Types in Swift:

Swift provides a rich set of data types for storing different kinds of information. Some of the fundamental data types in Swift include:

1. Int: Used to store integer values, such as 1, 2, -5, etc.

2. Double: Used to store floating-point values, such as 3.14, 2.5, -0.5, etc.

3. Float: Similar to Double, but with lower precision.

4. String: Used to store textual data, such as "Hello, World!".

5. Bool: Used to store Boolean values, such as true or false.

6. Character: Used to store single characters, such as 'a', 'b', 'c', etc.

Here is an example of declaring variables with different data types in Swift:

```swift
var age: Int = 30

var pi: Double = 3.14159

var isAdmin: Bool = true
```

```
var name: String = "John Doe"

var initial: Character = "J"
```

Arrays and Dictionaries:

In addition to the fundamental data types mentioned above, Swift also provides data structures such as arrays and dictionaries for storing collections of data.

Arrays are used to store an ordered collection of values of the same type. For example, an array of integers can be declared as follows:

```swift
var numbers: [Int] = [1, 2, 3, 4, 5]
```

Dictionaries, on the other hand, are used to

store unordered collections of key-value pairs. For example, a dictionary mapping strings to integers can be declared as follows:

```swift
var ages: [String: Int] = ["John": 30, "Alice": 25, "Bob": 35]
```

Type Inference:

In Swift, type inference allows the compiler to automatically determine the data type of a variable or constant based on its initial value. This can help reduce the amount of code needed to declare variables and make the code more concise.

Here is an example of type inference in Swift:

```swift
```

```
var number = 42  // Compiler infers number as
an Int

var message = "Hello, World!"  // Compiler
infers message as a String

```

By using type inference, you can write cleaner
and more readable code without sacrificing
type safety.

Optional Data Types:

Optional data types in Swift are used to
represent values that may or may not exist. An
optional is declared using the ? symbol after
the data type, indicating that the value can be
nil.

Here is an example of declaring optional
variables in Swift:

```swift
var optionalName: String? = "John Doe"
var optionalAge: Int? = nil
```

Optional data types are especially useful when dealing with values that may be missing or unknown, such as user input or network requests.

Conclusion:

In conclusion, Swift provides a wide range of data types for storing and manipulating information in a program. By understanding the fundamental data types in Swift, including variables, constants, arrays, dictionaries, and optional types, you can write more robust and efficient code. Whether you are developing an iOS app or a macOS application, mastering Swift's data types is essential for building successful software projects.

5.Collections: Arrays and Dictionaries in Swift

Collections: Arrays and Dictionaries in Swift

When working with Swift, one of the fundamental concepts you need to understand is collections. In Swift, collections are used to store multiple values of the same type. Two common types of collections are arrays and dictionaries. In this article, we will explore these two types of collections and how to use them in Swift.

Arrays in Swift

An array is a collection of values that are stored in a specific order. In Swift, arrays are declared using square brackets [] and can store values of the same type. For example, you can create an array of integers like this:

```swift
var numbers = [1, 2, 3, 4, 5]
```


You can also create an empty array and then append values to it later:


```swift
var names = [String]()
names.append("John")
names.append("Jane")
```


You can access elements in an array using subscript syntax. For example, to access the first element in the numbers array, you would do:

```swift

let firstNumber = numbers[0]

```

You can also modify the value of an element in an array using subscript syntax:

```swift

numbers[2] = 10

```

Arrays in Swift are mutable, which means you can change the values in an array after it has been created. You can also remove elements from an array using the `remove(at:)` method:

```swift

numbers.remove(at: 3)

```

Arrays in Swift also support a variety of useful methods such as `count` to get the number of elements in the array, `isEmpty` to check if the array is empty, `first` and `last` to get the first and last elements in the array, and `contains` to check if a certain value exists in the array.

Dictionaries in Swift

A dictionary is a collection of key-value pairs where each key is associated with a value. In Swift, dictionaries are declared using square brackets [] and can store key-value pairs of the same type. For example, you can create a dictionary of strings like this:

```swift
var fruits = ["apple": "red", "banana": "yellow", "orange": "orange"]
```

You can access the value associated with a key in a dictionary using subscript syntax. For example, to get the color of an apple, you would do:

```swift
let colorOfApple = fruits["apple"]
```

You can also modify the value associated with a key in a dictionary using subscript syntax:

```swift
fruits["banana"] = "green"
```

Dictionaries in Swift are also mutable, which means you can change the values associated with keys after the dictionary has been created. You can also add new key-value pairs to a dictionary like this:

```swift

fruits["grape"] = "purple"

```

You can also remove key-value pairs from a dictionary using the `removeValue(forKey:)` method:

```swift

fruits.removeValue(forKey: "orange")

```

Dictionaries in Swift also support a variety of useful methods such as `count` to get the number of key-value pairs in the dictionary, `isEmpty` to check if the dictionary is empty, `keys` and `values` to get an array of keys and values in the dictionary, and `contains` to check if a certain key exists in the dictionary.

Arrays vs Dictionaries

Arrays and dictionaries are both useful for storing and organizing data in Swift, but they serve different purposes. Arrays are ideal for storing a list of values that are ordered and accessed by index, while dictionaries are more suitable for storing key-value pairs that can be looked up by key.

When deciding whether to use an array or a dictionary, consider the type of data you need to store and how you need to access it. If you have a collection of values that need to be accessed in a specific order, an array is the best choice. If you have data that is associated with unique keys and needs to be looked up quickly, a dictionary is the way to go.

Arrays and dictionaries are essential collections in Swift that allow you to store and organize data efficiently. By understanding how to use arrays and dictionaries effectively, you can write more efficient and readable code in your Swift applications.

6.Optional type in Swift

In the world of programming, handling values that can be empty or nil is a common occurrence. In Swift, the optional type was introduced to handle such scenarios. In this article, we will explore what the optional type is, how it works, and how it can be used in Swift programming.

What is an optional type?

An optional type in Swift is a type that can either have a value or be nil, which indicates that it has no value. This is particularly useful when working with variables or properties that may or may not have a value at a given time.

In Swift, the optional type is denoted by appending a question mark "?" after the type. For example, a variable of type Int can be made optional by declaring it as "Int?". This indicates that the variable can either hold an integer value or be nil.

Handling optional values

When working with optional values in Swift, it is important to safely unwrap them to avoid runtime errors. There are several ways to safely unwrap optional values, including optional binding, nil coalescing operator, and optional chaining.

Optional binding is a common technique used to unwrap optional values safely. It involves checking if an optional value contains a non-nil value, and if so, assigning it to a new constant or variable. This can be done using if let or guard let statements.

```swift
var optionalValue: Int? = 10

if let value = optionalValue {
```

```swift
    // value is not nil, use it here
    print(value)
} else {
    // value is nil
    print("Value is nil")
}
```

Another way to handle optional values is to use the nil coalescing operator, denoted by "??" in Swift. This operator allows you to provide a default value in case the optional value is nil.

```swift
var optionalValue: Int? = nil
let value = optionalValue ?? 0
// value is now 0
```

Optional chaining is yet another technique used to safely access properties, methods, and subscript on optional values. This allows you to chain multiple optional values together without having to explicitly unwrap them.

```swift
class Person {

    var name: String?

}


var person: Person? = Person()

let name = person?.name

// name is an optional String

```

Using the optional type in Swift

The optional type is widely used in Swift

programming to handle scenarios where a value may or may not be present. This is particularly useful when working with user input, network requests, or external data sources where the presence of data is not guaranteed.

For example, consider a function that fetches user data from a server and returns an optional result. The optional type can be used to handle cases where the data may be missing or invalid.

```swift
func fetchUserData() -> String? {

    // Fetch user data from server

    let data = fetchData()


    if let user = data {

        return user.name
```

```
    }

    return nil

}
```

In this example, fetchUserData() returns an optional String, indicating that the user's name may or may not be available. By safely unwrapping the optional value using optional binding, we can access the user's name only if it is present.

Conclusion

The optional type in Swift is a powerful feature that allows developers to handle values that may be empty or nil. By safely unwrapping optional values using techniques such as optional binding, nil coalescing operator, and optional chaining, developers can avoid runtime errors and ensure their code behaves as expected.

The optional type in Swift is a valuable tool for handling optional values and ensuring robust and reliable code. By understanding how to work with optional values effectively, developers can write safer and more maintainable code in their Swift projects.

7.Flow control in Swift

Flow control is an essential aspect of programming in Swift, allowing developers to manage the flow of execution in their code. In this article, we will explore the different techniques and mechanisms for controlling the flow of execution in Swift, ranging from simple conditional statements to more advanced control structures.

Conditional Statements

One of the most basic forms of flow control in Swift is the conditional statement, which allows developers to run specific blocks of code based on certain conditions. The most common conditional statement in Swift is the if statement, which allows developers to execute a block of code only if a certain condition is true.

For example, consider the following code snippet:

```swift
let x = 10



if x > 5 {

    print("x is greater than 5")

}
```

In this example, the print statement will only be executed if the condition `x > 5` is true. Otherwise, the block of code inside the if statement will be skipped.

In addition to the if statement, Swift also provides the else and else if statements, which allow developers to define alternative blocks of code to be executed when the condition in the if statement is false or when additional conditions need to be checked.

```swift
let y = 4

if y > 5 {
    print("y is greater than 5")
} else {
    print("y is less than or equal to 5")
}
```

In this example, the else statement provides an alternative block of code to be executed when the condition in the if statement is false.

Switch Statements

Another powerful flow control mechanism in Swift is the switch statement, which allows developers to evaluate an expression against a set of possible values and execute different blocks of code based on the matching value.

```swift
let grade = "A"

switch grade {
case "A":
    print("Excellent!")
case "B":
    print("Good job!")
case "C":
    print("Average")
default:
    print("Try harder next time")
```

```
}
```

In this example, the switch statement is used to evaluate the value of the variable `grade` and execute the corresponding block of code based on the matching case. The default case is used to handle any values that do not match the defined cases.

Loops

Loops are another essential flow control mechanism in Swift, allowing developers to execute a block of code repeatedly until a certain condition is met. There are several types of loops available in Swift, including the for-in loop, while loop, and repeat-while loop.

The for-in loop is used to iterate over a sequence, such as an array or a range of values. The loop will iterate over each element in the sequence and execute the block of code inside the loop.

```swift
let numbers = [1, 2, 3, 4, 5]

for number in numbers {
    print(number)
}
```

In this example, the for-in loop is used to iterate over the elements in the array `numbers` and print each element to the console.

The while loop is used to execute a block of code repeatedly as long as a certain condition is true. The condition is checked at the beginning of each iteration, and if it evaluates to true, the block of code is executed.

```swift
var count = 0

while count < 5 {
    print(count)
    count += 1
}
```

In this example, the while loop is used to print the value of the variable `count` repeatedly until it reaches the value of 5.

The repeat-while loop is similar to the while loop, but the condition is checked at the end of each iteration. This ensures that the block of code inside the loop is executed at least once before the condition is checked.

```swift
var number = 1

repeat {
    print(number)
    number += 1
} while number < 5
```

In this example, the repeat-while loop is used to print the value of the variable `number` repeatedly until it reaches the value of 5.

Control Transfer Statements

Swift also provides control transfer statements, such as break, continue, and return, to control the flow of execution within loops and switch statements.

The break statement is used to exit a loop or switch statement prematurely, without completing all iterations or cases.

```swift
let numbers = [1, 2, 3, 4, 5]

for number in numbers {
    if number == 3 {
        break
    }
    print(number)
}
```

In this example, the break statement is used to exit the for-in loop prematurely if the value of the variable `number` is equal to 3.

The continue statement is used to skip the current iteration of a loop and continue to the next iteration.

```swift
let numbers = [1, 2, 3, 4, 5]

for number in numbers {
    if number % 2 == 0 {

        continue

    }

    print(number)
}
```

In this example, the continue statement is used to skip printing even numbers and continue to the next iteration of the for-in loop.

The return statement is used to exit a function prematurely and return a value to the caller.

```swift
func sum(a: Int, b: Int) -> Int {
    guard a >= 0 && b >= 0 else {
        return -1
    }
    return a + b
}
```

In this example, the return statement is used to exit the function prematurely if either `a` or `b` is negative, and return -1 to the caller.

Flow control is an essential aspect of programming in Swift, allowing developers to manage the flow of execution in their code. By leveraging techniques such as conditional statements, switch statements, loops, and control transfer statements, developers can effectively control the flow of execution and create robust and efficient programs. Understanding these flow control mechanisms and how to use them effectively is crucial for becoming a proficient Swift developer.

Overall, mastering flow control is key to writing clean, efficient, and maintainable Swift code. By understanding the various flow control mechanisms available in Swift and when to use them, developers can write more robust and flexible applications that meet their requirements.

8.Functions and tuples in Swift

One of the key features of Swift is its support for functional programming concepts, such as functions and tuples. In this article, we will explore how functions and tuples work in Swift and how they can be used to create more expressive and efficient code.

Functions are a fundamental building block of programming in Swift. A function is a reusable block of code that performs a specific task or calculates a value. Functions in Swift are defined using the "func" keyword, followed by the function name and a set of parentheses that contain any parameters that the function takes. For example, a simple function that adds two numbers together might look like this:

```swift
func add(_ a: Int, _ b: Int) -> Int {
```

```
    return a + b

}
```

In this example, the "add" function takes two integer parameters, adds them together, and returns the result as an integer. Functions can also have return types, which specify the type of value that the function will return. In this case, the "add" function has a return type of Int, indicating that it will return an integer value.

Functions in Swift can also have multiple return values using tuples. A tuple is a way to group multiple values together into a single compound value. Tuples are created by enclosing the values in parentheses and separating them with commas. For example, a function that calculates the sum and difference of two numbers might look like this:

```swift
func sumAndDifference(_ a: Int, _ b: Int) -> (Int, Int) {
    let sum = a + b

    let difference = a - b

    return (sum, difference)

}
```

In this example, the "sumAndDifference" function takes two integer parameters, calculates the sum and difference of the two numbers, and returns a tuple containing both values. The return type of the function is specified as (Int, Int), indicating that it will return a tuple containing two integer values.

Tuples in Swift can also be named, which can make the code more readable and maintainable. Named tuples are created by specifying labels for each value in the tuple.

For example, the previous function could be rewritten to use named tuples like this:

```swift
func sumAndDifference(_ a: Int, _ b: Int) -> (sum: Int, difference: Int) {

    let sum = a + b

    let difference = a - b

    return (sum: sum, difference: difference)

}
```

In this version of the function, the tuple return type is specified as (sum: Int, difference: Int), indicating that the tuple contains two integer values labeled "sum" and "difference". This can make it clearer to understand the meaning of each value in the tuple when using the function.

Functions in Swift can also be used as types, allowing them to be passed as parameters to other functions or stored in variables. This functional programming feature can be powerful for creating more flexible and modular code. For example, a function that takes another function as a parameter might look like this:

```swift
func applyOperation(_ a: Int, _ b: Int, operation: (Int, Int) -> Int) -> Int {

    return operation(a, b)

}


func add(_ a: Int, _ b: Int) -> Int {

    return a + b

}


let result = applyOperation(5, 3, operation:
```

    add)

```

In this example, the "applyOperation"
function takes two integer parameters, an
operation function that takes two integers and
returns an integer, and applies the operation to
the two input values. The "add" function is
passed as the operation parameter to calculate
the sum of the two numbers.

Overall, functions and tuples are powerful
features of Swift that can help developers
create more expressive and efficient code. By
understanding how functions and tuples work
and how they can be used in different
scenarios, developers can take advantage of
these functional programming concepts to
write clearer and more maintainable code in
their Swift applications.
```

9.The Classes in Swift

When it comes to programming in Swift, one of the key features that developers use to create more complex and dynamic applications is classes. Classes are a fundamental building block in object-oriented programming that allow developers to define custom data types and behaviors. In this article, we will explore what classes are, how they are used in Swift, and some best practices for working with them.

What are classes?

In Swift, a class is a blueprint for creating objects. Objects are instances of classes that have their own unique properties and behaviors. Classes define the structure and behavior of objects by specifying properties (variables) and methods (functions) that can be accessed and manipulated.

Classes are defined using the keyword "class" followed by the class name and a pair of curly braces. Inside the curly braces, developers can define properties and methods that describe the behavior of the class.

How are classes used in Swift?

Classes are used to create custom data types that model real-world objects or abstract concepts in a program. For example, a developer might create a "Car" class to represent different cars in a car dealership application. The class might have properties like "make," "model," and "year" that describe the car, as well as methods like "startEngine" and "accelerate" that define how the car behaves.

Once a class has been defined, developers can create instances of the class by using the class name followed by parentheses. These instances can then be used to access and manipulate the properties and methods of the class.

Classes can also inherit from other classes in Swift, creating a hierarchy of related classes. This allows developers to define common behaviors and properties in a superclass and then extend or override them in subclasses. This is known as inheritance and is a powerful tool for organizing and managing complex code.

Best practices for working with classes

When working with classes in Swift, there are some best practices that developers should keep in mind:

1. Encapsulation: Classes should encapsulate their data and behavior to prevent other parts of the program from directly accessing or modifying them. This is typically done by declaring properties as private or internal and providing public methods to interact with

them.

2. Inheritance: Use inheritance to create a hierarchy of related classes, but be careful not to create overly complex or deep inheritance trees. Inheritance should be used judiciously to avoid tight coupling between classes.

3. Composition: Instead of relying solely on inheritance, consider using composition to build more flexible and modular code. Composition allows developers to build classes from smaller, reusable components, making the code easier to read and maintain.

4. Protocol-oriented programming: Consider using protocols to define common behaviors and properties that can be adopted by multiple classes. Protocols provide a way to define interfaces and enforce behavior across different types without the need for traditional inheritance.

5. Memory management: Remember that classes are reference types in Swift, which means that instances are passed by reference rather than by value. Developers should be mindful of memory management and avoid creating retain cycles by using weak references or capture lists in closures.

In conclusion, classes are a powerful feature of Swift that allow developers to create custom data types and behaviors in their applications. By understanding how classes work and following best practices for working with them, developers can write more maintainable and scalable code. Classes are an essential tool for building complex software systems in Swift, and mastering them is key to becoming a proficient Swift developer.

For example, let's create a simple class called Person:

```swift
class Person {

var name: String

var age: Int


init(name: String, age: Int) {

    self.name = name

    self.age = age

}


func greet() {

    print("Hello, my name is \(name) and I am \(age) years old.")

}

}
```

In this example, we define a class called Person with two properties, name and age, and a method called greet. We also define an initializer, init, which is a special method that is called when an instance of the class is created.

To create an instance of a class, we use the class name followed by parentheses and any arguments required by the initializer. For example:

```
let person = Person(name: "John", age: 30)

person.greet()
```

This code creates an instance of the Person class with the name "John" and age 30, and then calls the greet method on that instance.

Classes in Swift also support getter and setter methods, which allow us to customize how properties are accessed and modified. We can use the keywords "get" and "set" to define custom behavior for properties.

For example, let's modify our Person class to include a computed property called isAdult:

```swift
class Person {

var name: String

var age: Int


init(name: String, age: Int) {

    self.name = name

    self.age = age

}


var isAdult: Bool {

    get {
```

```swift
        return age >= 18

    }

}


func greet() {

    print("Hello, my name is \(name) and I am \
(age) years old.")

}

}
```

In this example, we define a computed property called isAdult that returns true if the person is 18 years or older.

Classes in Swift can also have class methods and properties, which are associated with the class itself rather than with instances of the class. Class methods are defined using the keyword "class" before the method declaration, while class properties are defined using the keyword "static".

For example, let's add a class method to our Person class that prints a greeting to all people:

```swift
class Person {

var name: String

var age: Int


init(name: String, age: Int) {

    self.name = name

    self.age = age

}


var isAdult: Bool {

    get {

        return age >= 18
```

```swift
    }

}


func greet() {

    print("Hello, my name is \(name) and I am \
(age) years old.")

}



class func greetEveryone() {

    print("Hello everyone!")

}

}
```

To call a class method, we use the class name followed by a dot and the method name:

```swift
Person.greetEveryone()
```

This code calls the greetEveryone class method on the Person class.

Another important feature of classes in Swift is reference counting. Objects created from classes are reference types, which means that multiple variables can refer to the same object in memory. Swift uses automatic reference counting (ARC) to manage memory and ensure that objects are deallocated when they are no longer needed.

To avoid retain cycles, where objects reference each other in a way that prevents them from being deallocated, we can use weak and unowned references. Weak references are automatically set to nil when the object they refer to is deallocated, while unowned references assume that the object they refer to will never be nil.

Classes in Swift are a powerful tool for creating reusable code and organizing our applications. They allow us to define blueprints for creating objects, customize behavior with methods and properties, and manage memory using ARC. By understanding and utilizing classes effectively, we can write more maintainable and scalable code in Swift.

10.Constructors and Destructors in Swift

Initializers are used for setting up the initial values of an object when it is created, while deinitializers are used for cleaning up the resources used by an object before it is deallocated from memory.

Initializers in Swift are similar to constructors in other programming languages, but they are more flexible and powerful. They can have multiple parameters, optional values, and default parameter values. This allows developers to create objects with the desired initial state easily.

There are several types of initializers in Swift:

1. Default initializer: This is a special type of initializer that is created automatically by the compiler if no other initializers are provided. It initializes all properties to their default

values.

2. Memberwise initializer: This type of initializer takes parameters for each property in the class or structure and initializes them accordingly. It is convenient when all properties need to be initialized at once.

3. Custom initializer: Developers can create custom initializers to initialize objects in a specific way. They can have any number of parameters and logic to set up the object's initial state.

Deinitializers, on the other hand, are used to perform cleanup tasks before an object is deallocated from memory. They are declared using the `deinit` keyword and do not take any parameters. Deinitializers are called automatically by the system when an object is no longer needed.

It is important to note that deinitializers are

not commonly used in Swift because of the Automatic Reference Counting (ARC) mechanism, which handles memory management automatically. However, they can be useful for releasing external resources like files, sockets, or database connections.

Here is an example of how initializers and deinitializers are used in Swift:

```swift
class Person {
    var name: String

    init(name: String) {
        self.name = name
        print("Person \(name) is initialized")
    }
}
```

```swift
    deinit {
        print("Person \(name) is deallocated")
    }

}

var person1: Person? = Person(name: "John")
person1 = nil
```

In this example, we define a `Person` class with an initializer that takes a `name` parameter and a deinitializer that prints a message when the object is deallocated. When we create a `Person` object and set it to `nil`, the deinitializer is called automatically by the system to clean up any resources used by the object.

Initializers and deinitializers are essential components of Swift programming for setting up object states and cleaning up resources. Developers can use them to create custom initialization logic and ensure proper memory management in their applications.

11.Inheritance in Swift

Inheritance is a fundamental concept in object-oriented programming where a class can inherit properties and behaviors from another class. In Swift, inheritance allows a class to take on the characteristics of another class, enabling code reuse and promoting a hierarchical relationship between classes.

To declare a class that inherits from another class in Swift, you use the colon followed by the name of the superclass. For example, if you have a class called Animal and you want to create a subclass called Dog that inherits from Animal, you would declare it like this:

```
class Animal {
  var name: String
```

```swift
    init(name: String) {

        self.name = name

    }

}


class Dog: Animal {

  var breed: String


  init(name: String, breed: String) {

    self.breed = breed

    super.init(name: name)

  }

}
```

In this example, the Dog class inherits from the Animal class and adds an additional property called breed. The Dog class also has its own initializer that first initializes its own properties and then calls the superclass initializer using super.init.

Inheritance in Swift supports both single and multiple inheritance, which means a class can inherit from only one superclass but can conform to multiple protocols. This allows for greater flexibility in designing the class hierarchy and promoting code reuse.

One important concept to keep in mind when using inheritance in Swift is the principle of class initialization. When a subclass is initialized, it must ensure that all of its properties are initialized before calling the superclass initializer. This can be achieved by either providing default values for properties or by explicitly initializing them in the subclass initializer.

Another key point to consider when using inheritance in Swift is the use of the override keyword. This keyword is used to override a superclass method or property in the subclass. This ensures that the subclass implementation is used instead of the superclass implementation.

```
class Animal {

  func makeSound() {

    print("Animal makes a sound")

  }

}


class Dog: Animal {

  override func makeSound() {

    print("Dog barks")

  }

}
```

In this example, the Dog class overrides the makeSound method defined in the Animal class. When an instance of Dog calls the makeSound method, it will print "Dog barks" instead of "Animal makes a sound".

Inheritance in Swift promotes code reuse, which can lead to a more modular and maintainable codebase. By creating a class hierarchy that mimics the real-world relationships between objects, you can build a robust and scalable application that is easy to extend and maintain.

In conclusion, inheritance is a powerful feature in Swift that allows classes to inherit properties and behaviors from other classes. By carefully designing the class hierarchy and using the override keyword when necessary, you can create a flexible and scalable codebase that promotes code reuse and simplifies maintenance. Swift's support for single and multiple inheritance, along with its emphasis on class initialization, makes it a versatile language for building object-oriented applications.

The Inheritance in Swift with Examples

Inheritance is a fundamental concept in object-oriented programming languages, allowing classes to inherit properties and methods from parent classes. In Swift, inheritance is a powerful tool that helps programmers create reusable and efficient code. This article will explore the concept of inheritance in Swift, along with examples to demonstrate how it works.

In Swift, inheritance is achieved using the keyword "class" to define a new class that inherits from a parent class. The child class can access all the properties and methods defined in the parent class, known as the superclass. This allows for code reusability and makes it easier to maintain and update codebases.

For example, let's consider a superclass called "Animal" with properties like "name" and "age" and a method called "makeSound". Now, let's create a subclass called "Dog" that inherits from the "Animal" class. The "Dog" class can access all the properties and methods defined in the "Animal" class, but it can also define its own properties and methods.

```swift
class Animal {
    var name: String
    var age: Int

    init(name: String, age: Int) {
        self.name = name
        self.age = age
    }
```

```swift
    func makeSound() {

        // Abstract method

    }

}


class Dog: Animal {

    var breed: String


    init(name: String, age: Int, breed: String) {

        self.breed = breed

        super.init(name: name, age: age)

    }


    override func makeSound() {

        print("Woof woof")

    }

}
```

```

In the example above, the "Dog" class inherits from the "Animal" class and defines its own property called "breed" along with overriding the "makeSound" method to make the sound of a dog. This demonstrates how inheritance allows us to reuse and extend the functionality of existing classes.

Another important concept in inheritance is the "super" keyword, which is used to access the superclass's properties and methods from within a subclass. This allows for greater flexibility in creating subclasses that modify or extend the behavior of the superclass.

```swift
class Cat: Animal {
    var color: String

    init(name: String, age: Int, color: String) {

```swift
        self.color = color

        super.init(name: name, age: age)

    }


    override func makeSound() {

        print("Meow meow")

    }


    func purr() {

        print("Purring")

    }

}
```

In this example, the "Cat" class inherits from the "Animal" class and adds a property called "color" along with a method called "purr". The "makeSound" method is also overridden to make the sound of a cat. This demonstrates how subclasses can add new properties and methods while still inheriting the behavior of the superclass.

One important thing to note is that Swift does not support multiple inheritance, meaning a class can only inherit from one superclass. However, Swift allows for protocols and extensions to provide similar functionality as multiple inheritance.

Inheritance is a powerful feature in Swift that allows for code reusability and extensibility. By creating subclasses that inherit from a superclass, developers can efficiently organize and maintain their code while adding new functionality as needed. The examples provided demonstrate how inheritance works in Swift and how it can be used to create hierarchies of classes with shared behavior.

12. Polymorphism and Overriding in Swift

Polymorphism and overriding are two important concepts in object-oriented programming that allow programmers to create flexible and dynamic code. In Swift, a powerful and expressive programming language developed by Apple, polymorphism and overriding play a key role in designing and implementing complex software solutions.

Polymorphism is the ability of an object to take on different forms or types. In Swift, polymorphism is achieved through the use of inheritance and protocol-oriented programming. By defining classes and protocols, developers can create objects that can be treated as instances of their parent class or conforming to a protocol, allowing for code reuse and abstraction.

One of the key features of polymorphism in

Swift is method overriding. Method overriding allows a subclass to provide its own implementation of a method defined in its superclass. This means that a subclass can customize the behavior of a method inherited from its superclass, providing flexibility and extensibility in the code.

For example, consider a superclass called Shape with a method called draw(). A subclass called Circle can override the draw() method to draw a circle shape instead of the generic shape defined in the superclass. This allows for custom behavior to be implemented in the subclass while still benefiting from the structure and functionality provided by the superclass.

In Swift, method overriding is achieved by using the override keyword before the method definition in the subclass. This signals to the compiler that the method is intended to override a method in the superclass, preventing accidental errors and ensuring proper inheritance behavior.

Another important aspect of polymorphism in Swift is dynamic dispatch. Dynamic dispatch allows the runtime environment to determine which method implementation to use at runtime based on the actual type of the object, rather than the static type declared in the code. This enables polymorphic behavior and allows for flexibility in changing the behavior of objects at runtime.

In addition to method overriding, Swift also supports property overriding. Property overriding allows a subclass to provide its own implementation of a property defined in its superclass. This can be useful for customizing the behavior of properties or adding additional functionality to them in the subclass.

Overall, polymorphism and overriding in Swift provide powerful mechanisms for creating flexible and dynamic code. By leveraging these concepts, developers can design software solutions that are extensible, maintainable, and scalable. Swift's support for inheritance, protocols, method overriding, property overriding, and dynamic dispatch make it a versatile and expressive language for object-oriented programming.

polymorphism and overriding are essential concepts in Swift that enable developers to create sophisticated and adaptable software solutions. By understanding and effectively utilizing these concepts, programmers can leverage the full power of Swift's object-oriented programming capabilities and build robust and flexible applications.

For example, let's define a protocol called Animal:

```
protocol Animal {
```

```swift
    func makeSound()
}
```

Now, let's create two classes that conform to the Animal protocol:

```swift
class Dog: Animal {
    func makeSound() {
        print("Woof")
    }
}
```

```swift
class Cat: Animal {
    func makeSound() {
        print("Meow")
    }
}
```

We can now create instances of Dog and Cat and treat them as instances of the Animal protocol:

```
let dog = Dog()

let cat = Cat()


let animals: [Animal] = [dog, cat]


for animal in animals {

    animal.makeSound()

}
```

This code will output:

```
Woof

Meow
```

In this example, both Dog and Cat conform to the Animal protocol, allowing us to treat them as instances of the Animal type. This is the essence of polymorphism - objects of different classes can be treated as instances of a common type.

Overriding in Swift

Overriding in Swift is the ability for a subclass to provide its own implementation of a method that is already defined in its superclass. This allows subclasses to customize the behavior of inherited methods without changing the implementation of the superclass.

For example, let's create a class called Vehicle with a method called drive:

```swift
class Vehicle {
    func drive() {
        print("The vehicle is driving.")
    }
}
```

Now, let's create a subclass of Vehicle called Car that overrides the drive method:

```swift
class Car: Vehicle {
    override func drive() {
        print("The car is driving.")
    }
}
```

When we create an instance of Car and call the drive method, it will call the overridden implementation:

```swift
let car = Car()

car.drive()
```

This code will output:

```
The car is driving.
```

By using the override keyword, the Car class is able to provide its own implementation of the drive method, which is different from the one defined in the Vehicle class. This is how overriding allows subclasses to customize the behavior of inherited methods.

Polymorphism and overriding are powerful concepts in object-oriented programming that allow for flexibility and customization in the design of classes and their methods. In Swift, polymorphism is achieved through protocols and inheritance, while overriding allows subclasses to provide their own implementation of inherited methods.

By understanding and utilizing polymorphism and overriding, developers can create more flexible and scalable code that can easily adapt to changing requirements and use cases. By using the examples provided in this article, you can practice and master these concepts in Swift programming.

13.Extensions and Computed Properties in Swift

Extensions in Swift allow developers to add new functionality to existing types, such as classes, structures, enums, and protocols. This is particularly useful when working with types that are part of third-party libraries or frameworks, as it allows developers to add new methods, properties, and initializers without modifying the original source code.

Extensions can be used to add new methods to a type, modify existing methods, add new initializers, add computed properties, and more. For example, suppose we have a struct called Point that represents a point in a two-dimensional space:

```swift
struct Point {

    var x: Double
```

```swift
    var y: Double
}


extension Point {

    func distance(to point: Point) -> Double {

        let deltaX = self.x - point.x

        let deltaY = self.y - point.y

        return sqrt(deltaX * deltaX + deltaY *
deltaY)

    }

}
```

In this example, we have extended the Point struct with a new method called distance(to:) that calculates the distance between two points. This allows us to calculate the distance between two points using the following code:

```swift
let point1 = Point(x: 0, y: 0)

let point2 = Point(x: 3, y: 4)


let distance = point1.distance(to: point2)

print(distance) // Output: 5.0

```

Computed properties in Swift allow developers to define properties that are calculated on the fly, rather than being stored in memory. This is useful for properties that are derived from other properties or need to be calculated based on some logic. Computed properties can have a getter and setter, or just a getter if the property is read-only.

For example, suppose we have a class called Circle that represents a circle in a two-dimensional space:

```swift
class Circle {

    var radius: Double

    var area: Double {

        return Double.pi * radius * radius

    }


    init(radius: Double) {

        self.radius = radius

    }

}
```

In this example, we have a computed property called area that calculates the area of the circle based on its radius. This allows us to calculate the area of a circle using the following code:

```swift

let circle = Circle(radius: 5)

print(circle.area) // Output:
78.53981633974483

```

Extensions and computed properties are powerful features of Swift that allow developers to add new functionality and calculate properties on the fly. These features enable developers to write concise and expressive code, improve code reusability, and make code easier to maintain. By leveraging extensions and computed properties, developers can enhance the functionality of their applications and build more robust and scalable software solutions.

14.Swift protocols

In Swift, protocols are used to define a blueprint of methods, properties, and other requirements that a conforming type must implement. This allows developers to write more flexible and reusable code by defining common functionalities in protocols that can be adopted by multiple types. In this article, we will explore the various aspects of protocols in Swift and how they can be leveraged to improve code organization and maintainability.

Defining Protocols

To define a protocol in Swift, you use the protocol keyword followed by the name of the protocol. Inside the protocol body, you can specify the methods, properties, and other requirements that conforming types must implement. Here is an example of a simple protocol that defines a method for calculating the area of a shape:

```swift
protocol Shape {

    func calculateArea() -> Double

}
```

Any type that wants to conform to the Shape protocol must implement the calculateArea() method. This allows for different types of shapes, such as rectangles, circles, and triangles, to provide their own implementations for calculating the area.

Conforming to Protocols

To conform to a protocol in Swift, a type must implement all the requirements specified in the protocol definition. You can declare conformance to a protocol by listing the protocol name after the type name, separated by a colon. Here is an example of a struct that conforms to the Shape protocol:

```swift
struct Square: Shape {
    var sideLength: Double

    func calculateArea() -> Double {
        return sideLength * sideLength
    }
}
```

In this example, the Square struct conforms to the Shape protocol by providing an implementation for the calculateArea() method. The conforming type must adhere to the protocol requirements, but it can also provide additional methods and properties as needed.

Using Protocols for Composition

One of the key benefits of protocols in Swift is the ability to use them for composition. This means that a type can conform to multiple protocols, allowing it to encapsulate different behaviors and functionalities. This can help in building more modular and reusable code.

```swift
protocol Drawable {
    func draw()
}


struct Circle: Shape, Drawable {
    var radius: Double

    func calculateArea() -> Double {
        return Double.pi * radius * radius
```

```swift
    }

    func draw() {

        // Code for drawing a circle

    }

}
```

In this example, the Circle struct conforms to both the Shape and Drawable protocols. This allows instances of the Circle type to calculate their area and draw themselves on the screen, leveraging the functionalities provided by both protocols.

Protocol Inheritance

In Swift, protocols can also inherit from other protocols, enabling you to build more complex hierarchies of functionalities. When a protocol inherits from another protocol, it inherits all the requirements and constraints specified in the parent protocol.

```swift
protocol Named {

    var name: String { get }

}


protocol ShapeWithInfo: Shape, Named {

    // Additional requirements for shapes with a name

}
```

In this example, the ShapeWithInfo protocol inherits from the Shape protocol and adds an additional requirement for shapes to have a name property. Types that conform to the ShapeWithInfo protocol must implement both the calculateArea() method from the Shape protocol and the name property from the Named protocol.

Protocol Extensions

Swift allows you to extend protocols with default implementations for methods and properties. This can be useful for providing default behavior for protocols without the need for every conforming type to implement it.

```swift
extension Shape {
    func printDescription() {
        print("This is a shape.")
    }
}

struct Triangle: Shape {
```

```swift
    var base: Double

    var height: Double


    func calculateArea() -> Double {

        return 0.5 * base * height

    }

}


let triangle = Triangle(base: 5, height: 3)

triangle.printDescription() // Output: "This is a shape."

```


In this example, the Shape protocol is extended with a default implementation for the printDescription() method. This method is now available to all types that conform to the Shape protocol, including the Triangle struct, which can now call the printDescription() method without providing its own implementation.

Protocols are a powerful feature of Swift that enable developers to define blueprints of functionalities that can be adopted by multiple types. By using protocols, you can write more flexible and reusable code, improve code organization, and build hierarchies of functionalities with ease. Whether you are developing iOS apps, macOS applications, or any other project in Swift, understanding and utilizing protocols is essential for writing efficient and maintainable code.

15.Generics in Swift

Generics are an essential feature in the Swift programming language that enables developers to write flexible and reusable code. With generics, you can write functions, classes, and structures that can work with any data type. This allows you to write more efficient and concise code by avoiding code duplication and improving code maintainability.

One of the main benefits of using generics is type safety. With generics, you can specify the type of data that a function or class will work with, ensuring that the compiler catches any type mismatches at compile time rather than at runtime. This helps to prevent bugs and makes your code more robust.

Another advantage of generics is code reusability. By writing generic functions and classes, you can write code that can be used with a variety of data types without having to rewrite the code for each type. This can save you time and effort and make your codebase more maintainable.

In Swift, you can create generic functions by using angle brackets to define placeholders for types. For example, you can create a generic function that reverses an array of any type like this:

```swift
func reverse<T>(array: [T]) -> [T] {

    var result = [T]()

    for element in array {

        result.insert(element, at: 0)

    }

    return result

}
```

In this example, `T` is a placeholder for any type. When you call the `reverse` function with an array of integers, strings, or any other type, the compiler will infer the type based on the input argument.

You can also create generic classes in Swift. For example, you can create a `Stack` class that can work with any type like this:

```swift
class Stack<T> {

    var elements = [T]()

    func push(_ element: T) {

        elements.append(element)

    }
```

```swift
    func pop() -> T? {

        return elements.popLast()

    }

}
```

With the `Stack` class, you can create a stack
of integers, strings, or any other type by
specifying the type when you create an
instance of the class:

```swift
let intStack = Stack<Int>()

intStack.push(1)

intStack.push(2)

print(intStack.pop()) // Output: Optional(2)

let stringStack = Stack<String>()
```

```swift
stringStack.push("Hello")

stringStack.push("World")

print(stringStack.pop()) // Output: Optional("World")
```

Generics also play a significant role in Swift's standard library. Many standard library types, such as `Array`, `Dictionary`, and `Set`, are implemented using generics. This allows these types to work with any type of data and provides flexibility and efficiency in working with collections.

Generics in Swift are a powerful feature that allows you to write flexible, reusable, and type-safe code. By using generics, you can write functions and classes that can work with any data type, improving code maintainability and reusability. Generics are a fundamental part of the Swift language and are worth exploring to make your code more efficient and robust.

16.Enumerations and structures in Swift

Swift is a powerful and versatile programming language developed by Apple for iOS, macOS, watchOS, and tvOS. One of the core features of Swift is its support for enumerations and structures, which allow developers to create custom data types and organize their code in a more efficient and readable way.

Enumerations, also known as enums, are a way to define a group of related values in Swift. They enable developers to work with a fixed set of values and provide type safety to the code. Enums in Swift can have associated values, raw values, and can also have methods associated with them.

To declare an enumeration in Swift, you use the `enum` keyword followed by the name of the enumeration and the cases within curly braces. Each case represents a possible value that the enumeration can take. Here's an example of an enumeration representing the days of the week:

```
enum Day {
    case sunday
    case monday
    case tuesday
    case wednesday
    case thursday
    case friday
    case saturday
}
```

Enums can also have associated values, which allow you to attach additional information to each case. For example, you can define an enumeration to represent different types of messages:

```
enum Message {

    case text(String)

    case image(URL)

    case video(URL, duration: Int)

}
```

In this example, the `Message` enumeration has three cases, each with different associated values. This allows you to create instances of the `Message` enumeration with different types of messages.

Enums in Swift can also have raw values, which can be of any type that conforms to the `RawRepresentable` protocol. Raw values are used to provide a default value for each case in the enumeration. Here's an example of an enumeration with raw values:

```
enum Planet: Int {
    case mercury = 1
    case venus
    case earth
    case mars
    case jupiter
    case saturn
    case uranus
    case neptune
}
```

In this example, the `Planet` enumeration has

raw values of type `Int`, starting from 1 for the `mercury` case and incrementing by 1 for each subsequent case. You can access the raw value of an enumeration case using the `rawValue` property.

Structures, on the other hand, are a way to define custom data types in Swift. Unlike classes, structures are value types, which means that when you assign a structure instance to a new variable or pass it as a function argument, a copy of the instance is created. Structures in Swift can have properties and methods just like classes.

To declare a structure in Swift, you use the `struct` keyword followed by the name of the structure and the properties and methods within curly braces. Here's an example of a structure representing a point in a two-dimensional space:

```
```

```swift
struct Point {

    var x: Int

    var y: Int


    func distance(to point: Point) -> Double {

        let dx = Double(x - point.x)

        let dy = Double(y - point.y)

        return sqrt(dx * dx + dy * dy)

    }

}
```

In this example, the `Point` structure has two properties `x` and `y` representing the coordinates of the point. It also has a method `distance(to:)` that calculates the distance between two points using the Pythagorean theorem.

Structures in Swift can also have initializers to set up their initial state. You can define a default initializer with no parameters, memberwise initializer with parameters for each property, and custom initializers with additional logic. Here's an example of a structure with initializers:

```
struct Size {

    var width: Double

    var height: Double


    init(width: Double, height: Double) {

        self.width = width

        self.height = height

    }

}
```

In this example, the `Size` structure has a custom initializer that takes `width` and `height` parameters and assigns them to the corresponding properties.

Enumerations and structures are powerful features of Swift that enable developers to create custom data types and organize their code in a more efficient and readable way. By using enums to represent related values and structs to define custom data structures, developers can write more expressive and maintainable code. Swift's support for enumerations and structures makes it a versatile and user-friendly language for iOS and macOS development.

17.Functional programming in Swift

Functional programming is a programming paradigm that treats computation as the evaluation of mathematical functions and avoids changing state and mutable data. Swift, a popular programming language developed by Apple, supports functional programming paradigms and features. In this article, we will delve into the world of functional programming in Swift, exploring its key concepts, benefits, and how to implement functional programming techniques in Swift.

One of the core concepts of functional programming in Swift is immutability. Immutability refers to the properties of objects whose state cannot be changed after they are created. In functional programming, immutability is highly valued because it eliminates the risk of side effects and makes code easier to reason about and debug. In Swift, you can create immutable objects using the `let` keyword. For example:

```swift
let name = "Alice"
```

In the code snippet above, the variable `name` is declared as a constant using the `let` keyword, which means its value cannot be changed once it is assigned the value "Alice".

Another key concept of functional programming in Swift is first-class and higher-order functions. In Swift, functions are first-class citizens, which means they can be treated like any other value, such as integers or strings. This allows you to pass functions as arguments to other functions, return functions from functions, and store functions in data structures. Higher-order functions are functions that take other functions as arguments or return functions as results. The Swift standard library provides a number of higher-order functions, such as `map`, `filter`, and `reduce`, that make it easy to manipulate collections of data in a functional style. For example:

```swift
let numbers = [1, 2, 3, 4, 5]
let doubledNumbers = numbers.map { $0 * 2 }
```

In the code snippet above, the `map` function is used to transform each element of the `numbers` array by doubling it, resulting in the `doubledNumbers` array `[2, 4, 6, 8, 10]`.

Functional programming in Swift also emphasizes the use of pure functions. A pure function is a function that has no side effects and always produces the same output given the same input. Pure functions are easier to test, debug, and reason about because they do not depend on external state or mutable data. In Swift, you can create pure functions by ensuring that they do not modify state outside of their scope and by avoiding side effects such as network requests or file I/O. For example:

```swift
func square(_ x: Int) -> Int {

    return x * x

}
```

In the code snippet above, the `square` function is a pure function that takes an integer `x` as input and returns the square of `x` as output. The function does not depend on any external state or mutable data, making it pure.

Functional programming in Swift also promotes the use of recursion as a way to solve problems iteratively. Recursion is a technique in which a function calls itself to solve smaller instances of the same problem until a base case is reached. Recursion can be a powerful tool for writing concise and elegant code in Swift. For example, here is an implementation of the factorial function using recursion:

```swift
func factorial(_ n: Int) -> Int {
    if n == 0 {
        return 1
    } else {
        return n * factorial(n - 1)
    }
}
```

In the code snippet above, the `factorial`
function calculates the factorial of a given
integer `n` by recursively multiplying `n` with
the factorial of `n - 1` until the base case of `n
== 0` is reached.

One of the benefits of functional programming
in Swift is that it encourages the use of higher-
level abstractions and declarative code.
Functional programming enables you to
express complex computations in a concise
and readable way, making your code easier to
understand and maintain. By using higher-
order functions, pure functions, and
immutable data structures, you can write code
that is more modular, composable, and
testable.

Functional programming in Swift can also
lead to better performance and concurrency.
Functional programming techniques such as
immutability and pure functions can help

eliminate race conditions and other concurrency issues, making your code more reliable and scalable. By avoiding mutable state and side effects, you can write code that is easier to parallelize and optimize for performance.

Functional programming in Swift is a powerful paradigm that can help you write clear, concise, and maintainable code. By embracing concepts such as immutability, first-class and higher-order functions, pure functions, and recursion, you can leverage the full potential of functional programming in Swift. Whether you are a seasoned Swift developer or just starting out, exploring functional programming in Swift can open up new possibilities and help you become a more proficient and proficient programmer.

Functional programming in Swift is a

powerful programming paradigm that allows developers to write concise, readable, and maintainable code. By focusing on functions as the main building blocks of the code, functional programming encourages immutability, higher-order functions, and pure functions. In this article, we will explore the concept of functional programming in Swift and provide five examples to showcase its benefits.

1. Pure Functions:

One of the key principles of functional programming is the use of pure functions. A pure function is a function that always produces the same output for a given input and has no side effects. This means that pure functions do not modify external state or rely on external variables, making them easier to reason about and test. In Swift, we can create pure functions by avoiding mutating state and using constants instead of variables.

```swift
func add(_ a: Int, _ b: Int) -> Int {
    return a + b
}

let result = add(3, 4) // result is 7
```

In this example, the `add` function is a pure function because it takes two inputs and returns a value without modifying any external state. This simplicity and predictability make pure functions an essential aspect of functional programming.

2. Higher-Order Functions:

Another fundamental concept in functional programming is higher-order functions, which are functions that take other functions as parameters or return functions as output. In Swift, higher-order functions allow us to create powerful abstractions and improve the readability of our code. For example, the `map` function is a higher-order function that takes a transformation function and applies it to each element of an array.

```swift
let numbers = [1, 2, 3, 4, 5]
let squared = numbers.map { $0 * $0 } // squared is [1, 4, 9, 16, 25]
```

In this example, the `map` function takes a closure that squares each element of the `numbers` array. By using higher-order functions, we can write concise and expressive code that is easy to understand and maintain.

3. Filter:

Another useful higher-order function in Swift is `filter`, which allows us to select elements from an array that satisfy a given condition. By using `filter`, we can create more declarative and readable code that focuses on what we want to achieve rather than how to achieve it.

```swift

let evenNumbers = numbers.filter { $0 % 2 == 0 } // evenNumbers is [2, 4]

```

In this example, the `filter` function selects only the even numbers from the `numbers` array. By combining `filter` with other higher-order functions like `map` and `reduce`, we can perform complex operations on collections with minimal effort.

4. Reduce:

The `reduce` function in Swift is another powerful higher-order function that allows us to combine all elements of a collection into a single value. By providing an initial value and an accumulation function, we can perform operations like summing all elements, finding the maximum value, or concatenating strings.

```swift
let sum = numbers.reduce(0) { $0 + $1 } // sum is 15

let max = numbers.reduce(Int.min) { max($0, $1) } // max is 5
```

In this example, the `reduce` function is used to calculate the sum of all elements in the `numbers` array and find the maximum value. By leveraging `reduce`, we can simplify complex operations and write more expressive code.

5. Recursive Functions:

Functional programming also encourages the use of recursion to solve problems by breaking them down into smaller subproblems. By defining functions that call themselves with a smaller input, we can create elegant and efficient solutions to a wide range of problems. For example, we can implement the factorial function using recursion in Swift.

```swift
func factorial(_ n: Int) -> Int {
    if n == 0 {
        return 1
    } else {
        return n * factorial(n - 1)
    }
}

let result = factorial(5) // result is 120
```

In this example, the `factorial` function uses recursion to calculate the factorial of a given number. By embracing recursive functions, we can write code that is more expressive, modular, and scalable.

In conclusion, functional programming in Swift offers numerous benefits, including immutability, higher-order functions, and pure functions. By adopting functional programming principles, developers can write code that is more readable, maintainable, and testable. Through the five examples provided in this article, we have demonstrated the power of functional programming in Swift and highlighted its potential for creating robust and elegant solutions to a variety of problems. By leveraging pure functions, higher-order functions, recursive functions, and other functional programming concepts, developers can unlock new possibilities and improve the quality of their code.

18.Swift Closure

In programming, a closure is a self-contained block of code that can be passed around and used in your code. Swift, a powerful programming language developed by Apple, supports closures as a first-class citizen. Closures in Swift are similar to blocks in Objective-C and lambdas in other programming languages, but they offer more flexibility and power.

A closure in Swift captures and stores references to any constants and variables from its surrounding context. This allows the closure to access and modify the values of those variables, even if they are no longer in scope when the closure is executed. Swift closures are used in many scenarios, such as simplifying code, handling asynchronous operations, and creating higher-order functions.

There are three main types of closures in Swift: global functions, nested functions, and closure expressions. Global functions are defined outside any other function and can be called from anywhere in the code. Nested functions are defined within the body of another function and can capture values from their enclosing function. Closure expressions are unnamed blocks of code that can be assigned to variables or passed as arguments to functions.

One of the key features of closures in Swift is their ability to capture values from their surrounding context. This means that closures can store references to variables and constants from the scope in which they are defined. This makes closures powerful tools for creating code that is flexible and reusable.

For example, consider the following code snippet:

```swift
func makeIncrementer(forIncrement amount: Int) -> () -> Int {

    var runningTotal = 0

    func incrementer() -> Int {

        runningTotal += amount

        return runningTotal

    }

    return incrementer

}


let incrementByTen =
makeIncrementer(forIncrement: 10)

print(incrementByTen()) // 10

print(incrementByTen()) // 20

print(incrementByTen()) // 30
```

In this example, we define a function `makeIncrementer` that takes an integer parameter `amount` and returns a closure that increments a running total by that amount. The closure captures the running total variable from its surrounding context, allowing it to maintain state across multiple calls.

Closures in Swift can also be used to simplify code by serving as inline functions. Consider the following example:

```swift
let names = ["Alice", "Bob", "Charlie", "David"]

let sortedNames = names.sorted {

    $0 < $1

}

print(sortedNames) // ["Alice", "Bob", "Charlie", "David"]

```

In this example, we use a closure expression to define a sorting function that sorts an array of strings in ascending order. The closure is passed as an argument to the `sorted` method, allowing us to sort the array in-place without the need to define a separate sorting function.

Closures in Swift can also be used to handle asynchronous operations, such as network requests or file I/O. By capturing values from their surrounding context, closures can simplify the process of dealing with asynchronous code. Consider the following example:

```swift
func fetchData(completion: @escaping (Data?, Error?) -> Void) {

    DispatchQueue.global().async {

        // Simulate fetching data from a remote server
```

```swift
        let data = Data(repeating: 5, count: 10)

        DispatchQueue.main.async {

            completion(data, nil)

        }

    }

}


fetchData { data, error in

    if let data = data {

        print("Data received: \(data)")

    } else if let error = error {

        print("Error: \(error)")

    }

}
```

In this example, we define a function

`fetchData` that performs a simulated network request. The function takes a closure as a parameter, which is called when the data is successfully fetched. By capturing values from the surrounding context, the closure can access the data and error variables defined in the `fetchData` function.

Another common use case for closures in Swift is creating higher-order functions. Higher-order functions are functions that take other functions as arguments or return functions as results. Closures are often used to define these functions, allowing for a flexible and composable code structure.

Consider the following example of a `map` function implemented using closures:

```swift
func myMap<T, U>(_ array: [T], _ transform: (T) -> U) -> [U] {
```

```swift
    var result: [U] = []

    for element in array {

        result.append(transform(element))

    }

    return result

}


let numbers = [1, 2, 3, 4, 5]
let squaredNumbers = myMap(numbers) { $0 * $0 }
print(squaredNumbers) // [1, 4, 9, 16, 25]
```

In this example, we define a generic `myMap` function that takes an array of elements and a transformation closure as arguments. The closure is applied to each element in the array, resulting in a new array with the transformed elements.

Closures in Swift offer a wide range of possibilities for creating more expressive, efficient, and flexible code. By capturing values from their surrounding context, closures can simplify code, handle asynchronous operations, create higher-order functions, and more. Swift closures are a powerful tool that can help you write cleaner, more concise, and more maintainable code.

Closures in Swift are a fundamental feature of the language that provide a powerful mechanism for defining and working with blocks of code. Whether you are writing simple functions or complex asynchronous operations, closures offer a flexible and expressive way to encapsulate behavior and data. By understanding closures and their capabilities, you can take advantage of their power to write more efficient and readable code in Swift.

Index